Study Guide to Dealing with Difficult Parents

This Study Guide provides a variety of thought-provoking questions and activities to help you implement the concepts in the bestselling book, *Dealing with Difficult Parents, Second Edition*. For each chapter of the book, the Study Guide offers discussion questions, journal prompts, and group activities. You can work on these sections independently, in book studies, in professional learning communities (PLCs), in mentor sessions, and in professional development sessions.

As you work through this Study Guide, you'll learn how to make the book's strategies work for you, so that you can more effectively deal with parents in all kinds of challenging situations and help them get on your side to ensure students' success.

Other Eye On Education Books Available from Routledge
(www.routledge.com/eyeoneducation)

Dealing with Difficult Parents, 2nd Edition
Todd Whitaker and Douglas J. Fiore

A School Leader's Guide to Dealing with Difficult Parents
Todd Whitaker and Douglas J. Fiore

Dealing with Difficult Teachers, 3rd Edition
Todd Whitaker

What Connected Educators Do Differently
Todd Whitaker, Jeffrey Zoul, and Jimmy Casas

What Great Teachers Do Differently, 2nd Edition:
17 Things That Matter Most
Todd Whitaker

What Great Principals Do Differently, 2nd Edition:
18 Things That Matter Most
Todd Whitaker

School-Community Relations, 4th Edition
Douglas J. Fiore

Seven Simple Secrets, 2nd Edition:
What the BEST Teachers Know and Do!
Annette Breaux and Todd Whitaker

50 Ways to Improve Student Behavior:
Simple Solutions to Complex Challenges
Annette Breaux and Todd Whitaker

Teaching Matters:
How to Keep Your Passion and Thrive in Today's Classroom, 2nd Edition
Todd Whitaker and Beth Whitaker

Making Good Teaching Great:
Everyday Strategies for Teaching with Impact
Todd Whitaker and Annette Breaux

STUDY GUIDE TO DEALING WITH DIFFICULT PARENTS

Todd Whitaker and Douglas J. Fiore

Routledge
Taylor & Francis Group

NEW YORK AND LONDON

First published 2016
by Routledge
711 Third Avenue, New York, NY 10017

and by Routledge
2 Park Square, Milton Park, Abingdon, Oxon, OX14 4RN

Routledge is an imprint of the Taylor & Francis Group, an informa business

© 2016 Taylor & Francis

Library of Congress Cataloging-in-Publication Data
A catalog record for this book has been requested

ISBN: 978-1-138-96346-7 (pbk)
ISBN: 978-1-315-65876-6 (ebk)

Typeset in Palatino
by Apex CoVantage, LLC

Printed and bound in the United States of America by Publishers Graphics,
LLC on sustainably sourced paper.

Contents

Part Five: Increasing Parent Involvement

About the Authors

Dr. Todd Whitaker is a professor of education leadership at Indiana State University in Terre Haute, Indiana. Prior to coming to Indiana, he coached and taught at the middle and high school levels in Missouri. Following his teaching experience, he served as a middle school, junior, and high school principal. In addition, Dr. Whitaker served as middle school coordinator for new middle schools.

Dr. Whitaker has been published in the areas of principal effectiveness, teacher leadership, change, and staff motivation. He has written 40 books including *What Great Teachers Do Differently, Dealing with Difficult Teachers, Motivating & Inspiring Teachers* and *What Connected Educators Do Differently*. He is a highly sought after speaker for educators.

Todd is married to Beth, a former teacher and principal, who serves as director of the Faculty Center for Teaching Excellence at Indiana State. Beth and Todd have three children, Katherine, Madeline, and Harrison.

Dr. Douglas J. Fiore is currently the interim provost and dean at Ashland University in Ashland, Ohio. Prior to coming to Ohio, he served in faculty and leadership roles at Virginia State University, Virginia Commonwealth University, and the University of West Georgia. Dr. Fiore began his educational career teaching at the elementary school level in Indiana. Following his teaching experience, he served as an elementary school principal in two Indiana schools.

Dr. Fiore has been published in the areas of school-community relations, leadership theory, principal effectiveness, and school culture and has presented at numerous national and state conferences. He is the author of eight books including the best-selling textbook, *School-Community Relations*, as well as *Introduction to Educational Administration: Standards, Theories and Practice,* and *Six Types of Teachers: Recruiting, Retaining and Mentoring the Best.*

Doug is the proud father of three daughters, Meagan, Amy, and Katherine.

Introduction

This Study Guide is a tool to accompany the second edition of *Dealing with Difficult Parents* by Todd Whitaker and Douglas J. Fiore. A practical resource for educators examining how to communicate effectively with parents and how to deal with difficult parents, this book provides insights into transferable ways to get all parents on your side.

Note to facilitators: If you are conducting a book study group, seminar, or professional development event, this Study Guide also serves as a road map to help you organize your sessions and work with your group. It provides assistance to staff developers, principals, team leaders, college professors, and other educational leaders who are working with teachers as they develop their professional skills.

Dealing with Difficult Parents is a slender, but powerful book. It is not a book comprised of hard scientific data, detailed assessment rubrics, or esoteric theories. Instead, it is a book that clearly, concisely, and accurately informs teachers of how our most effective teachers deal with and collaborate with parents. Put simply, this text is a book that teachers can put to use, immediately. This guide, therefore, is written in a way that allows the participant not only to read and understand essential concepts, but also to take these back into their classrooms and schools and put them to immediate use.

To help you plan and organize your study sessions most effectively, each chapter or pair of chapters is divided into the following five sections:

- ◆ Key Concepts: These summaries of the key points of each chapter in the book will help you review and focus your thoughts.
- ◆ Discussion Questions: These questions and ideas help you learn more about yourself and your colleagues and will aid constructive conversation in the study group, workshop, or classroom setting.
- ◆ Journal Prompt: Based on the specific contents of each chapter, the journal prompts help you reflect, work through essential issues, and record what you have learned in writing.
- ◆ Group Activities: These activities allow you to explore concepts and ideas further by interacting with others in your study group, workshop, or classroom.
- ◆ Application: This section provides strategies for applying what you have learned in your classroom or school.

Part One

Today's Parents

Chapter 1: Dealing with Difficult Parents
An Overview
Chapter 2: Who Are These Guys?
Describing Today's Parents

🔑 Key Concepts

- Parents are parents, and they are not really that much different than they have ever been. Parents still want what is best for their children.

- It is essential to understand that 90-plus percent of the parents do a pretty good job in raising their children; 100 percent of the parents do the best they know how to do.

- We should never argue, yell, use sarcasm, or behave unprofessionally with parents.

- Student achievement increases as parents become more involved in their children's education.

- Of the 75 million children under the age of 18 living in U.S. households in 2014, 24.3 percent, or 18.1 million were living with their mother only.

- Children whose fathers are involved in their lives experienced fewer behavioral problems and score higher on reading achievement tests.

- In 2013, children represented 23.5 percent of the total population and 32.3 percent of people in poverty.

？ Discussion Questions

1. What is the most important idea communicated in these two chapters? How would you implement this idea in your work with parents?

2. Why is it important to understand parents and their possible hardships?

3. Why is it so important for us to consistently keep a positive focus when we work with parents?

4. In what ways is examining parent's life situations pointless? On the other hand, how can this knowledge be helpful to you as a teacher?

5. How are contemporary parents different from parents when we were children? In what ways are they similar?

Notes

✎ Journal Prompt

Think of the parent population in your school. Approximately what percentage of parents would you classify as really being difficult? What are some traits that these parents have in common? Is there any information in the first two chapters of this book that helps you understand these parents more clearly? Reflect on the effect that these difficult parents have on your dealings with all parents in your school.

_____

_____

_____

_____

_____

_____

_____

_____

_____

_____

_____

_____

_____

_____

_____

_____

_____

_____

_____

_____

_____

Chapter 1; Chapter 2

Parents in My Class

In small groups of three to five, ask participants to consider what the demographics of their students' parents look like. Have each group compare the data in Chapter 2 with what they have come to experience in your school. If there is not a perfect match, which there likely is not, then why is the information in Chapter 2 still pertinent? Have each group discuss how demographic information will help you more effectively deal with parents. Report to the large group your thoughts on the value of these two chapters.

Who You Are Is Where You Were When

Divide the group into teams based upon the decade in which they graduated high school. Decades with large concentrations of teachers, such as the 1990s can be divided into two groups to keep groups close in size. Distribute chart paper to each group. Have each group brainstorm responses to the following prompts: Who were your heroes when you were in high school? What did you do for fun when you were in high school? What were some no-nos when you were in high school? Who or what was cool when you were in high school? What were some family rituals you engaged in when you were in high school? After each group has had time to brainstorm responses, have them share their charts with the whole group. Notice how each question yielded radically different responses based on the decade in which participants graduated high school. What does this have to do with understanding parents? What does this tell us about our own biases and preferences? How can this knowledge help us understand differences between us and parents who may be of a different age?

Notes

✓ Application

The authors state that if you have any students that you just cannot tolerate any more, you feel like your patience bucket has run out, you can barely stand the thought of them walking into your classrooms tomorrow, there is one thing that you can do. There is one simple thing you can do that will give you a whole new perspective on that child. That is meet their parents.

Think about your current population of students, particularly those who give you the most challenges. Has meeting their parents helped you better understand them? Is there some universal truth to what the authors say on this topic? Make a list of your five most difficult parents. Similarly, make a list of your five most difficult students. See how closely your lists match. Share this with the whole study group at your next session.

Notes

Chapter 3: What's Wrong with These Parents Anyhow?

Key Concepts

- Parents have a great deal of information at their fingertips that is less than flattering about teachers and schools.

- Although most families fall somewhere in between the two extremes, families can be described as adult-centered or child-centered.

- Many of our parents are intimidated by us due to their own negative school experiences.

- Lots of schools are still mired in the traditional rituals we disguise as parent involvement opportunities.

- Due to cultural differences, many parents view communication with teachers as "checking up on them" and as an expression of disrespect.

❓ Discussion Questions

1. What is the most important idea communicated in this chapter?

2. What is your reaction to some of the book titles mentioned in this chapter? Are you aware of any other book titles that give a negative impression of teachers or schools?

3. In your school community, do you feel that there are more child-centered families or adult-centered families? Why do you feel as you do?

4. Do you see any examples of parents with negative school experiences clouding their judgment in your school?

5. Has your school made any progress in updating its structure for open houses or any other parent involvement programs? Why is it important to consider parent schedules when planning these events?

Notes

✒ Journal Prompt

Take a moment to reflect on ways in which you think parents may be different from those in previous generations. How many of these ways are the result of media influences or other information that parents have at their fingertips? Other than book titles, create a list of other sources of information that influence parent perceptions of our schools. Can we do anything to refute this information?

_____

_____

_____

_____

_____

_____

_____

_____

_____

_____

_____

_____

_____

_____

_____

_____

_____

_____

_____

_____

_____

Group Activities

Titles Really Make a Difference!

Choose one of the books mentioned in this chapter to read as a group. Or do a search and discover other titles that appear to create negative images of schools or teachers and read one of those. As a group, discuss whether or not the information in the book would be helpful to parents. Then talk about how accurately the title reflects the actual book content.

Creating Convenient Models

In groups of three to five, make a list of all opportunities that your school engages in to involve parents. Then, discuss the variables that have been considered in determining when these events are scheduled. For each event, imagine ways in which it could be scheduled to meet the needs of the highest percentage of parents in your school community. Report to the larger group how you think your school does at considering parents' schedules when creating and scheduling these events.

 Application

Examine a class list of students that you teach, and consider the extent to which their families appear to be adult-centered or child-centered. For many families, you will be making broad assumptions, but there will be some families for which you have evidence to support your opinion. Then think back to your own childhood. How would you describe your own family in terms of these characteristics? Consider the same information in light of your childhood friends' families. What patterns do you discover?

Part Two

Communicating with Parents

Chapter 4: Building Credibility
Everyone Wants to Associate with a Winner

🔑 Key Concepts

♦ If we establish trust with parents, then they allow us great discretion in the decisions we make involving their children.

♦ People view their local schools in a much more favorable light than they do schools on a national basis. Additionally, parents view the schools their children attend more positively than do community members without children in school.

♦ Regardless of how many people come to school events, we need to make sure that the ones that do attend feel special. Do not focus on the people who are not there. Instead, make sure that the ones who did come have a very positive feeling about their attendance. This builds credibility.

♦ Proactively communicating with parents early in the school year or before the year even starts gets you off to a powerful start. It's important to do this as early as possible.

♦ One effective thing to do is to touch base with a parent who had expressed concern over a situation a week or two later to ask how things were going. It is especially fun to do this when you know things are going better.

♦ In all classroom communications like newsletters or memos, the tone always needs to be positive and focused on those who are doing things right.

1. Why is it so important to establish trust with parents?

2. What are some examples from society that illustrate the fact that people want to associate with a winner?

3. What are some ways to motivate yourself and others in your school to make positive contacts with parents early in the school year? Are there ways to incentivize this?

4. The authors discuss how they used to give out their personal telephone numbers to parents. Is this a good idea? Why/why not?

5. Why is it important for classroom communications from teachers to focus on positive things people do instead of negative things?

Notes

✎ Journal Prompt

In this chapter, Whitaker and Fiore emphasize the importance of "establishing credibility." As evidence, they use the example of the decrease in Miami Heat fans nationally after LeBron James left the team. Think about ways in which your school establishes credibility and tries to appear to be a winner in your community. Have you consistently put positive information and news out to your community? Are there any missed opportunities to tell the good news?

_____

_____

_____

_____

_____

_____

_____

_____

_____

_____

_____

_____

_____

_____

_____

_____

_____

_____

_____

_____

_____

_____

Group Activities

All the News That's Fit to Print

Divide participants into teams based on grade level or subject taught. Give each group 20 minutes to create a positive newsletter about their area. This newsletter can include accomplishments, future plans, announcements of activities, etc. Do not worry about style or format, but simply ensure that everything written is positive, as outlined in Chapter 4. After 20 minutes, assemble as a large group and share your results. As a group discuss what would happen if this information all got combined and was sent home to parents. How would the perception of your school be altered?

Calling All Parents

In pairs, have participants discuss the success of your school's current open house or back-to-school night. In doing so, think about the relative attendance at the event. Is the attendance adequate, or would you like to see it improve? What are some ways that your school currently advertises the event to parents? Are there new ways that can be employed to improve attendance? After discussing this in pairs, share responses with the larger group. Create an action plan for improving attendance.

✓ Application

In this chapter, the authors discuss the importance of reaching out to the community. Make a list of ways in which you can make a positive impression throughout your community. Share the list you make with other members of your study group.

Create a specific plan for making a positive impression in your school community. In your plan, also include obstacles, followed by suggestions to overcome those obstacles. Even if you only arrive at a few steps to take to build credibility within your local community, create a timeline for initiating these steps.

Notes

Chapter 5: Taking Your Classroom Social

Key Concepts

♦ Used appropriately, social media is an incredible tool for communicating with lots of parents in a simple format.

♦ Smartphone users check Facebook, a tool that was once thought to be a passing fad, an average of 14 times a day. In addition, 81 percent of smartphone users check social media within 10 minutes of waking up.

♦ There are teachers across the country who are tweeting at the end of the school day short messages that parents can view pertaining to homework assignments, enriched learning opportunities, or important reminders.

♦ If parents don't typically, or ever, use the social media tool that you use, they quickly will once they realize that the tweets may feature their own kids and their accomplishments.

♦ Teachers can use Pinterest to pin pictures of their students engaged in a classroom activity or a field trip. They can post pictures taken from their smart boards so that students and parents can review lessons at home. They can post pictures of informational notes that previously were only communicated through copy paper and ink.

♦ Facebook allows you to post updates that parents can see immediately when they log onto their page. You can post information that pertains to homework, to clarify a new policy, or to explain how students are to complete an assignment. Parents can also send you a private message to ask questions about homework or to ask for a meeting.

? Discussion Questions

1. Which social media tools do you already use with parents? Are there tools that you can use effectively with information gleaned from this chapter?

2. What are some considerations in using Twitter as a communication tool with parents?

3. What are some things to consider before embarking on a meaningful social media campaign with parents?

4. How can you get parents to engage with you via social media?

5. What are five specific things that you can do with the various social media tools at your disposal to communicate effectively with parents?

Notes

✏ Journal Prompt

Make a list of all social media tools that you currently use in your personal life. For each one of the tools on your list, reflect on which ones you believe you could use as a communication tool with parents. What are some things to consider before using these tools? Do you know teachers whom you could consult in using these tools effectively? Write a plan for more effectively using varied social media tools to communicate with parents.

_____

_____

_____

_____

_____

_____

_____

_____

_____

_____

_____

_____

_____

_____

_____

_____

_____

_____

_____

_____

Group Activities

Accentuate the Positive!

In this chapter, the authors give some examples of ways in which social media can be incorporated into a communication plan for parents. Distribute five slips of paper to each member in your study group. Ask each member to list an outcome on each slip that can be expected when the use of social media with parents is expanded upon. Collect the slips and categorize each of them as positive or negative. Distribute the collaborative lists of positive and negative outcomes to each member of the study group. For each negative outcome, discuss how they can be eliminated. You should be left with only a list of positive outcomes of using social media in your communication plan. Distribute this positive list to all members of the study team.

Things to Consider

Have participants read the bulleted list in the section called "Initial Considerations." In small groups, ask them to rank the list in order of importance for effectively utilizing social media tools for communicating with parents. Volunteers can then add considerations to this list not presented by the authors.

✓ Application

Complete the survey below as a way to self-reflect on your individual use of social media. Respond to each statement with the following one to four ranking.

Social Media Practices Self-Assessment

4 = Almost always; 3 = Frequently; 2 = Occasionally; 1 = Never

_____ 1. I use social media tools in my personal life.
_____ 2. I use social media as a tool to communicate with parents.
_____ 3. I pay close attention to the security settings of social media tools that I use.
_____ 4. I involve students in my use of social media as a parent communication tool.
_____ 5. I use social media daily.
_____ 6. I communicate with parents daily.
_____ 7. I vary the methods that I use to communicate with parents.

Chapter 6: Positive Communication with Parents
An Ounce of Prevention
Chapter 7: Listen, Learn, and Cultivate

🔑 Key Concepts

- If parents do not hear good news from us, they may never hear good news about schools and teachers. Thus, it is critically important that we consistently initiate positive contact with parents.

- Calling parents with positive messages while they are at work makes it much easier when you later have to call them at work with negative news. It also provides great positive publicity to the workplace.

- Praise is most effective when it is authentic, specific, immediate, clean, and private.

- It is important to be very consistent in the way we interact with parents. By having a specific approach with how we always initiate contact allows for a more level and diplomatic conversation regardless of what kind of news was shared.

- If teachers only send home notes when students are failing or misbehaving, for example, then parents will quickly begin to dread hearing from teachers.

- Schools can be safe and friendly at the same time. Safety is important, but we should not sacrifice the sense that we really are welcoming our visitors.

1. Why is it important to initiate positive contact with parents?

2. What are two important reasons why we suggest that you call parents at work when you have positive information to share?

3. Ben Bissell shares five things that make praise most effective. Are these things equally important? Do you feel that one or two of these five are really the most significant ones to remember?

4. What are some reasons the authors give for reaching out to parents with positive news before you are in a position to deliver negative news?

5. Consider the message that greets parents when they arrive at your school building. Is this message a positive and inviting one? How would you make it more positive?

Notes

✎ Journal Prompt

In Chapter 6, the authors suggest particular scripts to use for when you make positive telephone calls to parents. The authors stress the importance of ensuring that you have a consistent script that you use each time. Create a script that would work best for you in your situation. Use the authors' suggested script as a guide, but make whatever modifications you think fit your school situation best.

Creating a Positive Referral Program

Working in groups of two to five, create a positive referral program that can be instituted at your grade level or in your instructional team. Think about specific steps that you could take to ensure that this plan provides opportunities for recognizing positive things that students do. Write the details of your plan on chart paper and share the charts with other groups. Discuss commonalities and differences between these plans.

A Welcoming Environmental Audit

In pairs, take a walk around your school building, including the exterior grounds and parking lots. Throughout your walk, focus all of your attention on the welcoming messages—actual or implied—that are present or lacking. Try to see your school environment through the eyes of somebody who rarely, if ever, comes to the school building. Examine signage, entry points, and even decorations. Then as a large group, brainstorm a list of all observations. Go through the list and identify areas that do not appear to be inviting to parents or guests. Make a plan to fix these areas and to make your school seem welcoming and inviting from the moment people step on the grounds.

Notes

✓ Application

Upon returning to your classroom, engage in self-reflection about your relationships with parents. Identify opportunities that may exist for you to reach out positively on a more regular basis. List as many opportunities as you can in which you can make positive phone calls, send positive notes, or share positive messages through newsletters or social media. Create a plan for improvement in this regard, and be prepared to share it during the next session.

Notes

Part Three

Soothing the Savage Beast

Chapter 8: Initiating Contact with Parents

🔑 Key Concepts

♦ If you do not already have an established relationship with a parent, it is important to consider heavily whether or not you should use email to communicate. Oftentimes, the telephone is the best tool to use.

♦ If a parent uses email to communicate negatively with you, always respond via telephone. Email allows a degree of anonymity, and your more personal response will put you back in control.

♦ Do not threaten calling parents. Just call the parents. Anytime we threaten to call parents the students now have an opportunity to go home and prep their parents against us.

♦ If a group of students is disrupting instruction, consider calling the parent who has the most influence over their child first. Rather than risk having a group of parents and students against us by calling several parents, eliminating negative behavior one student at a time will have the most desirable effect.

♦ If there is negative news to communicate, it is best to do so before the parent is at their "peak of ready."

♦ Understand that some adults—just like children—will use crying as a weapon.

---

1. What are some advantages that phone calls have over email with challenging parents?

2. What is one possible negative reason why some parents may choose to use email when communicating with us?

3. Oftentimes, we hear teachers threatening to call students' parents. Why is this a bad idea? Why do the authors say, "Do not threaten calling parents. Just call the parents"?

4. If an entire class or a group of students is misbehaving or failing to do their work, how do you decide how many parents to call? How do you know who should be called first?

5. How do the authors suggest we should respond to parents who use crying as a weapon?

Notes

Think about the concept of the "peak of ready." Consider times in which you waited for a parent to be at the "peak of ready" before you contacted them. How did that situation go? Write down all of the reasons why you are at a disadvantage by waiting until this point to initiate contact with a parent. What are the potential pitfalls of waiting? Although you may be too nervous to initiate contact yourself, also list the advantages that you realize by reaching out before the parent is at the "peak of ready."

_____

_____

_____

_____

_____

_____

_____

_____

_____

_____

_____

_____

_____

_____

_____

_____

_____

_____

_____

_____

Acting It Out

Divide participants into pairs and have each pair prepare a skit involving a telephone conversation with parents. In the skits, half of the groups should show a scenario in which the teacher called the parent to inform them of a situation that they had not yet learned of from their child. In the other half of the groups, the skit should involve a telephone conversation between teacher and parent in which the parent is at the "peak of ready." After all skits have been completed, have the group make a list of all advantages that arise when a teacher calls a parent long before the parent is at the peak of ready.

Communicating with Parents

Write each of the following eight statements on an index card (if there are more than 16 participants, create additional statements that probe teacher beliefs about how best to communicate with difficult parents or in difficult situations):

1. It is much easier to email a parent than it is to call.
2. When you choose to email a parent, you inadvertently put them in control.
3. Parents often want a feeling of anonymity by emailing.
4. Anytime we threaten to call parents, the students now have an opportunity to go home and prep their parents against us.
5. If you call parents and the students have not prepped them in advance, you are much more likely to have the upper hand. It takes eight times longer to unlearn something than it does to learn something.
6. If we have five challenging students, our goal is to go from five to four; then to go from four to three; then three to two, etc. There is very little chance of going from five to zero in one fell swoop.
7. By initiating contact with parents, you can make contact when you are ready, not when they are ready.

Ask participants to stand in two concentric circles, facing a partner. Give each participant in the inner circle one of the index cards. Have them ask their partners in the outer circle to discuss their level of agreement with the statement on the index card, based on a scale of one ("strongly disagree") to four ("strongly agree").

After two minutes, have partners in the outer or inner circle rotate to the next partner. (The group leader may call rotation numbers, "Rotate three ahead.") Continue for three or four rotations.

Collect the index cards and give them to the participants in the outer circle. Repeat the process three or four more times with the roles of speaker and listener reversed. Debrief the process by asking participants to share their thoughts on how these statements may or may not define "students first" teachers and teaching.

Notes

Application

Upon returning to your classroom, reflect on the applications of the term "peak of ready." We already know the value of making contact with parents when you, not they, are at the peak of ready. For this week, consider this concept as you work with students and colleagues. When delivering bad news, are there advantages to you being at the peak of ready? Is this different when it comes to student learning? How can you tell if students are at the peak of ready to learn? Since learning is a positive occurrence, can any analogies be made when you are delivering positive news to parents? In such times, is it good for the parents to be at the peak of ready too? Prepare to discuss your thoughts on the application of this concept at your next study group session.

Notes

Chapter 9: Never Let 'Em See You Sweat
Chapter 10: What If the Parent Is Right?

🔑 Key Concepts

♦ Despite the fact that difficult parents sometimes make us feel nervous or anxious inside, it is important that when dealing with a difficult parent, you never let 'em see you sweat.

♦ If difficult parents are able to intimidate you, not only do you risk losing the respect of those around you, but also you increase the odds that you will cave in to the difficult parents and yield to their requests.

♦ In dealing with difficult parents, you should never feel the need to always be right. It should never be about winning or losing.

♦ If the parent is upset about something that you have done wrong, you should apologize.

♦ By contacting parents who you know are upset before they contact you, a great deal of their anger can be diffused. If instead we hide our heads in the sand and hope that the parents won't call us, then nine times out of 10 all we do is give the parents more time to become even angrier.

❓ Discussion Questions

1. What are some steps that we can physically take when we are feeling nervous or intimidated by a difficult parent?

2. How can a change in proximity help reduce the aggressiveness of an angry parent? What are some considerations regarding the speed and extent to which we should change proximity?

3. When you have done something wrong, why is it important to contact parents before they can contact you?

4. What are some advantages to appreciating parents who bring injustices to your attention?

Notes

✏ Journal Prompt

Reflect on the section of Chapter 10, entitled "The Incorrect Grade." Have you ever been in a situation in which a student was given an errant grade? Write down how you have handled that in the past. Are there new ways that you have learned from this chapter to employ if you are in that situation again? Evaluate the language in the example used by the authors. Would that language work for you? If alternatives are necessary, write down how you might have communicated what the authors said in this chapter.

Group Activities

The Sorry Actors

Divide into groups of three to five, and create a skit that illustrates a situation in which teachers should apologize to parents. The skit should include either an apology in person or one on the phone. As each skit is performed, the larger group should take note of the specific words used in the apology. Furthermore, attention should be paid to the body language, vocal tone, and body movement. Discuss whether or not the teacher's apologizing seems genuine. Then, talk about what is at risk if an apology does not come across as genuine.

Attention

Have each person write down one situation in which a parent brought something to his or her attention, perhaps a complaint, which actually was helpful. In other words, each person should think of a time in which a parent raised an issue in which an injustice was perceived, and the parent actually was right. Have each study group member report this issue to the larger group. Look for patterns in the kinds of issues parents most often have brought to the attention of teachers. If patterns are present, consider as a group whether or not there are steps you can take to avoid these situations from occurring in the future.

 Application

Take the concepts from these two chapters and see how they can apply to your work with students. For one week, ask students to be extra vigilant in politely pointing out injustices. Respond to these injustices in the same manner with which you reply to parents. See if there is any positive impact on your classroom climate. At the very least, pay attention to how students feel when they are receiving apologies for what they perceive as injustices. Bring your observations to your next group study session to debrief.

Chapter 11: The Best Way to Get in the Last Word . . .
Chapter 12: Do You Feel Defensive? If So, Something Is Wrong

🔑 Key Concepts

- The single best diffuser in any situation is to apologize.

- Being able to say, "I am sorry that happened," is universally applicable language that allows you to tell the truth, support others, and still be sorry.

- Often, even irate parents want someone to listen to them more than they want someone to solve their problems.

- We truly believe that you do not control anyone's behavior by rules. We believe that everyone knows what the "rules" in life are and attempting to effect inappropriate behaviors with rules makes no sense.

- If we are making all of our decisions based on what is best for students, then we should never feel defensive.

- If the first contact we make with parents can be to call and ask for their help, we may be able to avoid situations where parents ask us why they did not know earlier and then we feel the need to defend our actions.

1. Why is it often difficult for teachers to apologize to parents?

2. What are the risks if we allow rudeness, arrogance, impatience, or sarcasm to drip into our voice when we attempt to apologize?

3. Explain the point that the authors are trying to make when they critique "No Smoking" and "Shoplifters Will be Prosecuted" signs.

4. What is meant by the Chapter 12 subsection, "You Can't Make Sense Out of No Sense"?

5. Why do the authors suggest that teachers call parents to ask for help before waiting until there is a problem? How will calling with a request for help first be of any assistance?

Notes

Take some time to think about situations in which it would be most effective to tell parents that you are sorry something happened. In your journal, reflect on how this approach would help you. When you consider the power of using these words to apologize, you quickly recognize that an apology does not require you to actually take responsibility for anything. Create a script for an actual situation you have been in that would have loaned itself to this approach.

_____

_____

_____

_____

_____

_____

_____

_____

_____

_____

_____

_____

_____

_____

_____

_____

_____

_____

_____

_____

Circle of Bad News

Arrange participants into two concentric circles with partners facing each other. Have the people in the inner circle relate an example of negative news that they have had to communicate to parents. The person in the outer circle should listen carefully and offer suggestions for how this news could more easily and effectively be delivered. After a few minutes, have the inner circle rotate two places to the right. Repeat the activity, this time asking the people in the outer circle to share their negative scenarios. Repeat once or twice. Then, have the entire group share what they learned. Did most participants share similar stories? What were the most useful strategies for delivering bad news?

A Sign of the Times

Post this sign on the board or chart paper:

SHOPLIFTERS WILL BE PROSECUTED

Ask participants how many of them have seen this sign or a similar one in stores. The authors mention that signs such as this one seldom are effective. As a group, discuss the extent to which you agree with the authors' assertion. Now, consider the signs greeting visitors at your school. Ask participants if they feel that these signs produce the desired result or if the desired result is obtained more because people already know the rules and are generally compliant. Discuss whether or not the wording of the school greetings can be more friendly while still producing the desired results.

Notes

✓ Application

Make a conscious decision, upon your return to your school or classroom, to proactively communicate negative situations that inevitably face you, your students, and their parents. Decide to use the telephone or face-to-face conferences for such situations, and develop a script for communicating bad news. After doing this for one month, record in your study guide any changes you have noticed in your own perspective or those of parents with whom you have dealt. Are you feeling a tide shift in how parents react to negative news? Are you thinking of other venues in your life in which this approach may be useful?

Notes

Part Four

Dealing with Parents in Difficult Situations

Chapter 13: Delivering Bad News

🔑 Key Concepts

♦ A standard we should establish with parents is that the worse the news, the more thought and effort we need to put into delivering it.

♦ If students carry notes home from teachers to their parents, they get to share their point of view with the parents before the teacher does.

♦ Teachers need to develop a consistent approach when contacting any parent for any reason. Each phone call home whether it is for a positive or a negative situation should start out the same.

♦ Sometimes, before even responding to a negative comment by a parent, it is best to ignore it and see if it the parent brings it up again.

♦ When a parent brings up a negative situation of which you don't have first-hand knowledge, it's sometimes better to shift the focus toward an event or occurrence that you did witness and can speak clearly about.

1. What are some reasons why we, as teachers, dislike having to deliver negative news to parents?

2. Do you agree with the premise, "The worse the news, the more effort we use" as it pertains to working with parents? Why? Why not?

3. Why might an effective teacher choose to call parents on the telephone when delivering bad news? Why is it so important to call the parents before they learn of the situation from their child?

4. Why is the simple act of saying, "I am sorry that happened" such a powerful tool?

5. How should you deal with a parent who says that their child never lies to them?

Notes

Imagine (or draw on your own experience) a situation in which parents are visibly upset with you about an incident at school involving their son or daughter (a bad grade, a demeaning comment allegedly made about the child, a punishment that they consider unjust, etc.). Write about this situation and how it would play out if you had contacted the parent before they learned of the situation from their son or daughter. Compare this with what would happen if you sent an email. Finally, write about what might happen if the parent contacted you about the situation first.

The Legal Eagle

Post this scenario on the board or chart paper:

> A PARENT CALLS OR EMAILS YOU AT LEAST ONCE
> A MONTH TO OBJECT TO SOMETHING THAT THEIR CHILD
> CLAIMS HAS HAPPENED IN YOUR CLASSROOM

Ask participants how many of them have experience with this scenario. List adjectives on the board that explain these feelings. Ask participants how they have handled this scenario in the past. As a group, contrast the responses with the ideas and examples given in Chapter 13. As a group, discuss how you will handle these types of parents in the future. Will you still feel those feelings that you previously described on the board?

A Bad News Triangle

Arrange the entire group into smaller groups of three. Ask each group to create a real or imagined scenario in which a teacher needs to deliver bad news to a parent. Have one person in each group role-play as the teacher and one as the parent, while the third member is the silent observer. At the conclusion of each role-play, the silent observer should give feedback to both participants regarding their effectiveness based on the information from Chapter 13. Switch roles until each group member has had a chance to play each role. As a large group, share observations about the ease or challenges of delivering bad news.

✓ Application

Interview a teacher or principal who has not read this book (perhaps someone from another school). Ask them how they typically deliver bad news to parents. Also, ask them if they ever avoid delivering bad news in the hopes that the parents never will find out. Share with them some of the ideas you have learned in this chapter and in previous chapters that will assist you in delivering bad news more effectively. Teach them why it rarely works to avoid delivering bad news to parents and why it's always best to do so when you are at the peak of ready. Finally, encourage them to develop specific scripts for when they find themselves in these situations.

Notes

Chapter 14: But I Did Get a Good Deal
Examining the Car Salesperson

Key Concepts

- Understanding this dynamic of "feeling" as though you got a good deal can be very beneficial in effectively interacting with parents.

- Oftentimes as educators, we reduce negative consequences in our own mind before we share them with students or parents. Sometimes, manipulating this reality can be beneficial.

- Remembering the basic concept of making people feel like they were treated fairly, or maybe even that they got a good deal, can go a long way in developing and maintaining positive relations.

- Many belligerent parents feel very resentful toward authority. Working to get on their side can be very beneficial.

❓ Discussion Questions

1. Is it manipulative to try and ensure that people feel as though they've gotten a good deal? Why? Why not?

2. Why do the authors suggest that judgment is needed before embarking on the techniques in this chapter? What are the risks of overusing the car salesperson technique?

3. Even before you ever heard of the car salesperson technique, have you ever helped students or parents feel like they had gotten a good deal? Instinctively, why is this approach important?

4. List as many scenarios as you can in which convincing a parent that they got a good deal would be useful.

Notes

✏ Journal Prompt

For two of the scenarios that you created in question four of the previous discussion questions, write a script that explains how you would speak with the parent and show them that they got a good deal. What does it feel like to offer these deals? In your journal, share any levels of comfort or discomfort that this important approach brings you.

_____
_____
_____
_____
_____
_____
_____
_____
_____
_____
_____
_____
_____
_____
_____
_____
_____
_____
_____
_____
_____
_____

Group Activities

I Really Did Get a Good Deal

Mimic the car-buying scenario described by the authors. Begin by asking how many participants have purchased or leased a new car within the past five years. Of those who raise their hands, ask how many of them believe that they got a good deal. Count the hands that go up. Make a list of all behaviors that car salespeople engage in to make people feel as though they have gotten a good deal. Then, ask participants for examples in which these same behaviors can be used in the teaching profession.

Acting It Out

Divide participants into groups of five to seven and have each group prepare a skit involving an opportunity in which a student, a group of students, or a parent is given a good deal. In the skits, each group should include a rule violation that either was not witnessed by the teacher or involves the teacher communicating to a very defensive parent. In each presentation, have the "teacher" deal effectively with these situations by clearly illustrating the "bargain" that the student received.

 Application

Spend a week recording any and all opportunities in which you offer a student or a parent a good deal. For each situation that arises, consider the result and also consider what you would have done prior to focusing on this technique. At your next study group session, come prepared to share your observations from this week. As a large group, spend 10 minutes debriefing and explaining what it felt like to offer good deals.

Notes

Chapter 15: What If They Use the "F" Word—Fair?
Chapter 16: Focus on the Future

🔑 Key Concepts

♦ One challenge that every educator faces is when there is an accusation that something is not fair.

♦ One of the first things that we need to do in order to diminish the amount of "that's not fair" comments is to be fair. Not only to be fair, but to be perceived as being fair.

♦ Being calm, relaxed, confident, and assertive all at the same time is important in discussing fairness with parents. Practicing the specific words in the dialogue can allow you to be able to pull them out of your tool kit at the most opportune times.

♦ Shifting the focus from the present—which we might not all agree about—to the future can allow for the development of a common understanding.

♦ Making sure that we listen, remain calm, and show a genuine interest in a parent's concerns are essential in order to develop credibility and build positive relations.

♦ In disagreements, getting all sides to realize the benefit to looking forward to something we can influence is much more empowering then only centering on things that we cannot control.

? Discussion Questions

1. What is the most important idea communicated in these two chapters? How would you implement this idea in your classroom? Are there any ideas in these chapters with which you disagree?

2. Consider the oft-used comment, "Perception is reality." How does this comment relate to fairness?

3. The authors quote Gary Phillips (1997), "Treating unequals equally is no justice." How does this quote relate to fairness?

4. Why do the authors recommend that the more the parents are hung up on the "fair" issue, the more the word should be used in your response? Do you agree?

5. What are the most obvious advantages of moving parents away from a discussion about the past, which we do not agree on, to the future?

6. Why do the authors point out the value of making sure that we listen, remain calm, and show a genuine interest in a parent's concerns? In what ways does this behavior help us?

✏ Journal Prompt

Reflect on the issue of fairness. We all know that fairness is so important to students, but have you realized how much it means to parents also? Using examples from the text as a guide, write down two more examples from your past, as a teacher, a parent, or a student, in which the perception of fairness was central to the issue at hand. How was the feeling of fairness restored?

Group Activities

Working with Mrs. Johnson

Think about the examples with Mrs. Johnson from Chapter 16. Divide the participants into small groups and have them discuss the following questions: What were some deliberate statements that the teacher made to keep Mrs. Johnson focused on the future? Why are these statements preferential to leading with the potential consequences Amber faces? How likely is it that Mrs. Johnson will be cooperative with the teacher? Have you faced situations similar to this one? Have each group share their ideas with the whole group.

Using the "F" Word

Divide participants into groups of three to five, and give each team a sheet of chart paper. Ask participants to create a picture or group of pictures that symbolize the "F" word, fair. The only binding rule is that no words are to be used in their graphic representation. Allow 15 to 20 minutes for the pictures to be completed. Once completed, each group should share with the large group what they drew and why they drew it.

 Application

Choose one concept from these two chapters that you find laudable as well as transferable to your own work with parents and incorporate it into your daily professional life. Record your progress toward this goal in your journal over the next few weeks, noting specific occasions when you utilized this concept with parents. Be prepared to share what you have written during a future study session.

Notes

Part Five

Increasing Parent Involvement

Chapter 17: Understanding Parent Involvement

🔑 Key Concepts

- The more parents are involved in our schools, the more they understand the struggles and challenges that teachers face today.

- Throughout the past few decades, there have been numerous reports and a large body of research stating that parent involvement is a critical factor in the success of students.

- Many of our students' parents either had negative school experiences themselves, are so unfamiliar with American culture that they do not want to get involved, or they feel unsure about the value of their contributions.

- Teachers need to work constantly to build parents' confidence that their school encounters will result in positive interactions and success for their child.

- No longer are schools seen as institutions existing solely for the purpose of imparting knowledge to children. Rather, modern schools are tasked to meet cultural, social, and educational needs of families as well.

1. In what ways does involving parents in schools help them understand and support the work done by teachers?

2. Compare/contrast parents of previous generations with parents of today. What are some key differences in how they support schools and teachers?

3. What happens when parents are made to feel uncomfortable? What happens when parents feel comfortable?

4. The National Coalition for Parent Involvement in Education points out the importance of staff development for teachers and administrators to enable them to work effectively with families and with each other as partners in the educational process. How can you accomplish this at your school?

5. Does your school schedule activities with enough flexibility to allow participation of diverse groups of parents? Why? Why not?

Notes

In your journal, evaluate the National Coalition for Parent Involvement in Education's keys to successful parent involvement programs offered in this chapter. How many of them are present in your school? Do you agree that all are beneficial? What will you do to incorporate them into your school?

_____

_____

_____

_____

_____

_____

_____

_____

_____

_____

_____

_____

_____

_____

_____

_____

_____

_____

_____

_____

_____

_____

Comparing Parents

There is no question that parents have changed, as has their involvement in their children's education. Divide the group into teams of four to five, and give each group a chart or sheet of paper with the following table on it:

	Previous Generations	Contemporary Parents
Work Life		
Home Life		
Involvement		
School Manners		

Have each group fill in the chart including the differences in work life, home life, involvement in their children's education, and ways in which parents behave in school and interact with teachers. Have each group share their chart with the entire group, as you look for patterns in all of the responses.

Dealing with Difficult Parents

As a summary of all previous chapters, consider the following five tips. Divide the study group into five sections and assign one of the following tips for dealing with difficult parents to each section:

1. Approach difficult situations and difficult parents with an attitude of respect and a willingness to listen. Remember that you and the parents have one thing in common: the desire for their children to succeed.
2. Address specific complaints with ideas about what you and the parents can do together to find a solution.
3. Exercise empathy—always take some time to walk in the parents' shoes and try to gain an understanding of their perspective.
4. Express an attitude that is pleasant, not defensive or negative.
5. Understand the value of parent involvement and the positive role it plays in student achievement.

Each group should examine their assigned tip and report back to the large group their thoughts on the suggestion. Have each group brainstorm situations in which they could employ the technique and role-play a situation in which they practice the suggestion. After each group has presented their assigned tip, ask volunteers to share other effective ways of dealing with difficult parents. Remind participants that great teachers do not fall into the trap of arguing with parents or responding defensively.

 **Application**

Upon returning to your school, reflect on the many ways in which your school involves parents and celebrates their involvement. Similarly, consider ways in which your school misses opportunities for parental involvement. Write an assessment for your school administration. Include in this assessment rationale for any suggestions you make for improvement. This can be done individually or in groups. The important outcome is to ensure a thorough evaluation of your school's efforts at keeping diverse parents involved.

Notes

Chapter 18: Increasing Parent Involvement at School
Chapter 19: Increasing Parent Involvement at Home

🔑 Key Concepts

- The connections that are built when teachers take deliberate action to transform their schools into communities are strong and necessary.

- Several structural difficulties exist in some schools that pose additional challenges to keeping parents involved.

- Although unintended, we often alienate parents with our safety structures, which effectively make visitors feel unwelcome.

- There are numerous ways in which teachers can keep parents involved in their children's education while respecting the fact that many of them are unable or unwilling to physically come to the school.

- In addition to the important task of creating positive learning environments at home and speaking positively about school, parents in many school communities are asked to supplement their children's learning at home.

- Informing parents of their importance in reading to their children, monitoring their homework, and discussing expectations regarding conduct and citizenship are among the most significant ways that schools can involve parents at home.

? Discussion Questions

1. What are some structural changes in your school that inhibit parent involvement?

2. The authors often note the fact that many parents had negative school experiences when they were children. Why is this important? What can teachers do to overcome the feelings that have arisen as a result of these experiences?

3. List all of the ways that your current school, and previous school if pertinent, involved parents. Which of these had the most positive impact on student learning? Which had the least impact?

4. If you could tell all parents about three things that you would like them to do at home to support your efforts and to help their children learn, what would those three things be?

5. As the authors have suggested throughout this book, it is important for parents to feel welcome at your school. What are some things that you can do to increase the welcoming feeling without negatively impacting safety?

Notes

✎ Journal Prompt

Consider the National PTA Standards for Family-School Partnerships from Chapter 18. Write the standard that you think is most impactful from your teaching perspective. Which standard do you think carries the most importance? List ways that you and others in your school could act on and strengthen this standard in your school. Prepare to share these thoughts at the next group study session.

_____

_____

_____

_____

_____

_____

_____

_____

_____

_____

_____

_____

_____

_____

_____

_____

_____

_____

_____

💬 Group Activities

Clarifying Your Parent Core

After reviewing the core beliefs about parents listed below, ask individuals to think about additional core beliefs not mentioned in the text that are essential components of establishing strong relationships and collaborating successfully with parents. Have each participant write two to four additional core beliefs they value as educators. Have participants pair up to share these additional beliefs. Invite volunteers to share these with the whole group.

Parents do the best job they know how to do.
Dealing with difficult parents is essential because it improves learning for students.
Proactively communicating with parents yields much better results than does being reactive.
Parents really want what's best for their children.

Homework

Divide participants into small groups, and ask each group to brainstorm things that parents can do at home to support teaching and learning. As this is a brainstorming session, have participants write down every point that is expressed. After several minutes, have each group share their list with the whole group. Assign a facilitator to record new ideas, note redundancies, and turn the list into a collective, collaborative example of ideas that could be shared with parents.

   Ask each individual to take the list back with them to their classrooms, and continue to refine it before turning it in to the leader by a specified date. The leader should then organize and write the list in a manner that can be displayed or shared with parents.

✅ Application

As a reflective exercise, consider all of Chapter 18's suggestions for involving parents. Consider, too, all of the examples that you have tried or witnessed to involve parents in education. Create a parent involvement plan for your classroom. This plan should have specified outcomes and should clearly delineate what you hope to accomplish with parents and why you find it important to partner with them. Seek out input from parents to uncover whether or not anybody is available, as you may need them. Perhaps, you can post these thoughts on social media to generate some responses. Create from this a cogent plan for parent involvement that you can begin implementing.

Notes